GETTYSBURG: THEN AND NOW

TOURING THE BATTLEFIELD WITH OLD PHOTOS
1863–1889

by
William A. Frassanito

THOMAS PUBLICATIONS
Gettysburg PA 17325

Printed and bound in the United States of America

Published by THOMAS PUBLICATIONS
P.O. Box 3031
Gettysburg, Pa. 17325

ISBN-1-57747-003-6

Cover design by Ryan C. Stouch

ACKNOWLEDGEMENTS

The author would like to thank several individuals for their special contributions to this study. They include Elizabeth Sheffer, who in 1988 gave me her collection of 25 rare, cabinet-sized (roughly 5 x 8) glass-plate negatives originally produced by Levi Mumper. Fred Sherfy alerted me on December 1, 1995, to the existence of the previously unknown photograph taken by Peter Weaver on the day of the dedication of the National Cemetery. Carolyn S. Stauffer, of the Hanover Area Historical Society, kindly allowed me to copy and reproduce that outstanding image.

Thanks are likewise due to Robin Stanford, for permission to use her rare Weaver stereo of the Union breastworks on Culp's Hill; as well as to Mary Lou Schwartz, for permission to use her equally rare Weaver stereo of the East Cavalry Battlefield. Elwood W. Christ, of the Adams County Historical Society, kindly made available a portion of the modern panorama he produced from the cupola of the original edifice at the Lutheran Theological Seminary; and Timothy H. Smith provided assistance by researching some obscure details concerning William H. Duttera.

KEY TO PHOTO CAPTIONS AND CREDITS

Each historical photograph reproduced in this study is accompanied by a multi-part caption that includes, in the following order: an assigned photograph number; my title for the image; the name of the firm or photographer who produced the original negative; the original format of issue; the original or contemporary issue number; the date of the negative; and the source for the image reproduced in this book. The abbreviations for the photographic sources are as follows:

ACHS: Adams County Historical Society
GNMP: Gettysburg National Military Park
HAHS: Hanover Area Historical Society
LC: Library of Congress
Schwartz: Mary Lou Schwartz
Spectrum: Pennsylvania College yearbook, 1907
Stanford: Robin Stanford
USAMHI: US Army Military History Institute
WAF: William A. Frassanito

Unless otherwise specified, the caption descriptions will refer to the original photograph, and not to the modern companion.

INTRODUCTION TO THE TOUR

In compiling this photographic tour of the Gettysburg Battlefield, then and now, it was my desire to provide the modern visitor with a sampling from the rich body of photographic documentation produced at Gettysburg during the first quarter-century following the battle. While my previous books, *Gettysburg: A Journey in Time* (1975) and *Early Photography at Gettysburg* (1995), go into great detail about the individual views and the various series recorded during the 1860s, I have expanded my time frame for this study to include a number of subjects that are immensely popular today, but were simply ignored by the earliest cameramen.

At the same time, I deemed it essential to provide a representative selection of classic views from the 1860s, including a number of death studies. Because many of these important scenes, together with companion views not reproduced here, are discussed more fully in my previous books, I have included a "notes" section for those who may wish to learn more about the when, why, how, and by whom one of the greatest battlefields in the world was documented when the field still looked essentially as it did at the time of the battle.

For the convenience of the modern visitor, the 50 early photographs which comprise this then-and-now journey across the Gettysburg Battlefield have been arranged in a sequence roughly corresponding to the current National Park Service tour route.

Because the cameramen of 1863-1889 selected their points of perspective without regard to official tour routes or one-way avenues, diversions from the current route will occasionally be necessary for those who would like to visit the original camera positions in the order in which events occurred during the battle. Most of the scenes recorded in the town, for instance, are clustered together at the end of the tour, simply because the modern tour route bypasses much of the borough. Of course, the modern visitor is perfectly free to visit the 50 camera sites in any sequence he or she might desire. The accompanying map clearly locates all 50 sites.

The modern photographs were deliberately recorded when the trees were bare, because the dense foliage of today often obscures many vistas that were unobstructed by foliage more than a century ago. While every effort was made to take the modern views from the original camera positions, this was occasionally not possible due to the subsequent development of the area, or to the ephemeral nature of the original camera platform.

Additional installments of *Gettysburg: Then and Now*, are currently being planned. Anyone who has rare photographs they would like to be considered for inclusion may contact the author in care of Thomas Publications.

THE BATTLE OF GETTYSBURG

The three-day battle at Gettysburg began just west of town on the morning of July 1, 1863. Confederate General Robert E. Lee's Army of Northern Virginia, on its second great invasion of the Civil War, was by then dispersed throughout the region as General George G. Meade's Union Army of the Potomac was heading northward in search of the invading force. The fighting commenced as a chance encounter between Union cavalry and a Confederate reconnaissance-in-force.

Within a short while, the widely scattered elements of both armies were set in motion toward Gettysburg, the struggle growing in magnitude as the various units reached the field. Initially, Union forces successfully defended the open ground west of town, to be joined on their right flank (north of town) by additional troops who arrived at midday. But because more Confederate reinforcements were able to reach Gettysburg that day than Union reinforcements, the Union lines west and north of town began to collapse at about 4 P.M. Retreating through the town, the Union forces rallied on Cemetery Hill.

Not until July 2 would both armies be present on the field in their entirety, the defensive lines of the Army of the Potomac ultimately extending in a three-mile arc from Culp's Hill on the right, around to Cemetery Hill, then southward along Cemetery Ridge, and terminating in the vicinity of Little Round Top on the left. Late in the afternoon of July 2, the Army of Northern Virginia launched its assaults from Seminary Ridge against the Union left, attacking in succession: Little Round Top and Devil's Den, the Wheatfield, the Peach Orchard, and the Emmitsburg Road. Near dusk, the Confederate forces struck both Culp's Hill and Cemetery Hill. Despite some success in these poorly coordinated attacks, especially against the advanced positions on the Union left, Lee's troops failed to break either Union flank.

On the afternoon of the final day's fighting, July 3, 1863, Lee tried once again; this time with a massive frontal assault against the Union center on Cemetery Ridge. The failure of this desperate attack (since known as Pickett's Charge), together with the failure of Lee's attempt at a coordinated cavalry action three miles east of town, effectively ended the battle of Gettysburg. Remaining on the field through July 4, Lee commenced his retreat to Virginia that night.

A major turning point in the four-year Civil War, Gettysburg also holds the tragic distinction of being one of the bloodiest battles in American history. During the three days of fighting, which involved approximately 160,000 soldiers, some 51,000 would become casualties, i.e., killed, wounded, captured, and missing. On November 19, 1863, President Abraham Lincoln here delivered his immortal Gettysburg Address at the dedication of the National Cemetery for the Union dead.

PHOTOGRAPHING THE BATTLEFIELD, 1863-1889

Gettysburg, without question, was the most photographed battlefield in the 19th century. Not only did the battle's magnitude immediately capture the attention of the entire nation, but the field's relative closeness to several major photographic centers, i.e., Washington, New York, and Philadelphia, made the field readily accessible to some of the country's most prestigious cameramen. And because the Gettysburg area had its own indigenous photographers, local firms would continue to record the field from 1863 through the present.

Although no cameramen were able to document the actual battle, Washington photographer Alexander Gardner and two assistants, Timothy H. O'Sullivan and James F. Gibson, were taking death studies on the southern portion of the field as early as the third day after the fighting. (Only Gardner's series would include scenes depicting human dead.) Shortly after Gardner's coverage, Frederick Gutekunst would arrive from Philadelphia; the famous M. B. Brady arrived from New York within several days of Gutekunst.

From August-November 1863, various portions of the field were documented by local cameramen, Charles and Isaac Tyson of Gettysburg, and Peter S. Weaver of nearby Hanover, Pa. As the war continued elsewhere in 1864-1865, few new negatives were produced at Gettysburg. But by 1867, the demands of a budding tourist industry would prompt these local firms to renew their coverage in earnest, with some 250 new scenes being produced between 1867-1869.

With their inventories well stocked by 1870, local firms spent the next several years updating their most popular subjects—while making only a token effort to document subjects which had previously escaped the attention of all cameramen. Though such features as Cemetery Hill, Culp's Hill, the Round Tops, Devil's Den, and the town itself remained perennial favorites during this early period, other significant sites went largely ignored. The latter category included the first day's field north and west of town; the Wheatfield; the Peach Orchard; the Emmitsburg Road; and most surprisingly, the climactic site of Pickett's Charge.

But with the 1880s came the period of memorialization, wherein literally hundreds of monuments were placed on the field by Union veterans. Many miles of avenues were constructed, and new railroad connections to Gettysburg made the battlefield more accessible than ever. Correspondingly, this explosion of interest led to an unparalleled increase in the production of new scenes. The local firms of William H. Tipton and Levi Mumper were more than willing to provide tourists and veterans with souvenirs of the newly memorialized field, including subjects that had never before been photographed.

I have chosen to use 1889 as the closing date for this study to enable me to include a number of views from a group of original Mumper negatives I acquired several years ago. These scenes provide rare glimpses of features that went unphotographed prior to the period of memorialization, and help to round out this visual tour of "Gettysburg, then and now."

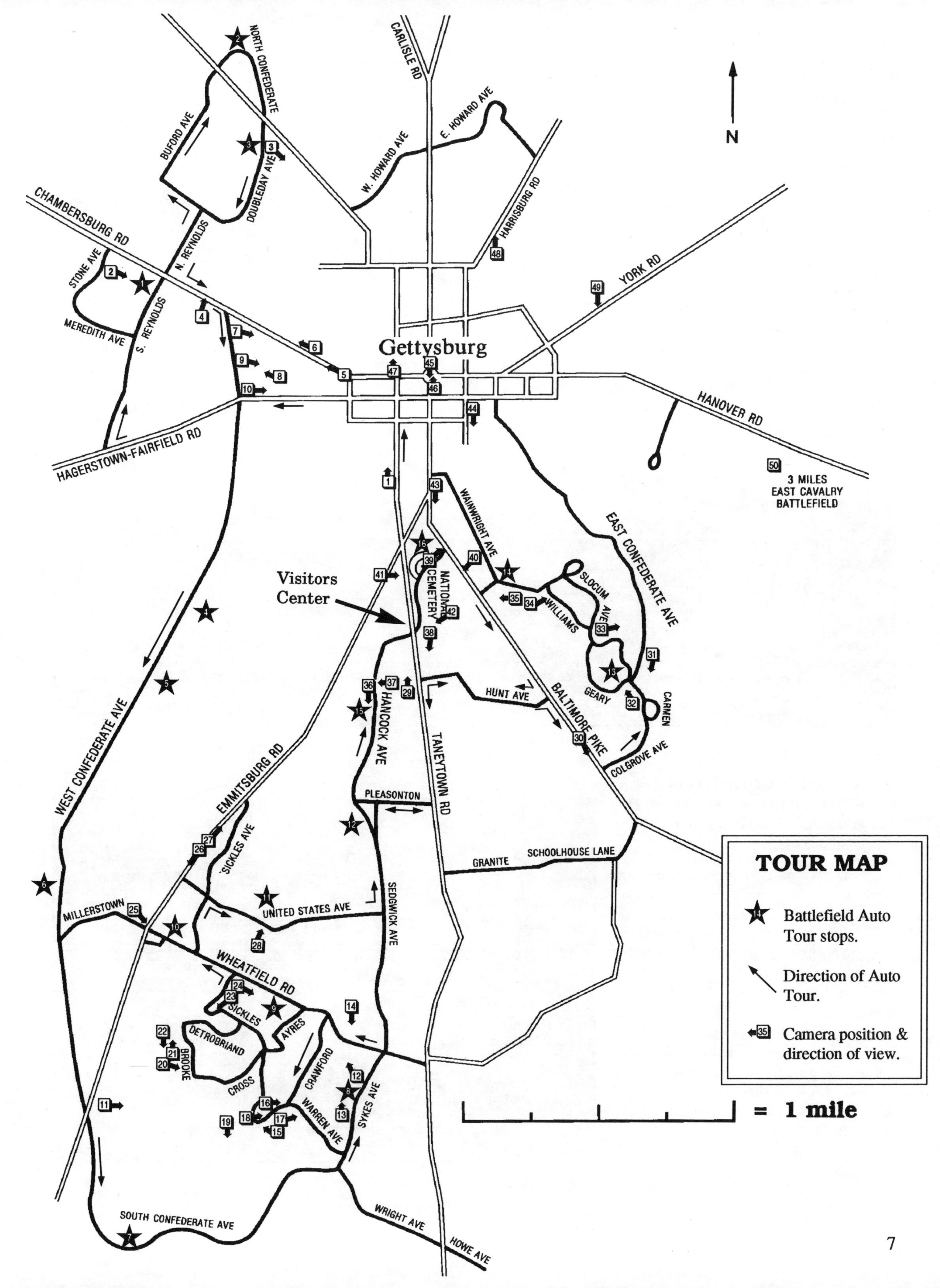
TOUR MAP
Battlefield Auto Tour stops.
Direction of Auto Tour.
Camera position & direction of view.
= 1 mile
N
Gettysburg
Visitors Center
NORTH CONFEDERATE
CARLISLE RD
E. HOWARD AVE
W. HOWARD AVE
BUFORD AVE
DOUBLEDAY AVE
HARRISBURG RD
CHAMBERSBURG RD
N. REYNOLDS
S. REYNOLDS
STONE AVE
MEREDITH AVE
YORK RD
HANOVER RD
HAGERSTOWN-FAIRFIELD RD
3 MILES EAST CAVALRY BATTLEFIELD
WAINWRIGHT AVE
EAST CONFEDERATE AVE
NATIONAL CEMETERY
SLOCUM AVE
WILLIAMS
GEARY
CARMEN
HUNT AVE
BALTIMORE PIKE
COLGROVE AVE
HANCOCK AVE
TANEYTOWN RD
WEST CONFEDERATE AVE
EMMITSBURG RD
PLEASONTON
SICKLES AVE
SEDGWICK AVE
GRANITE
SCHOOLHOUSE LANE
MILLERSTOWN
UNITED STATES AVE
WHEATFIELD RD
SICKLES
DETROBRIAND
AYRES
BROOKE
CROSS
CRAWFORD
WARREN AVE
SYKES AVE
SOUTH CONFEDERATE AVE
WRIGHT AVE
HOWE AVE

1) SOUTH WASHINGTON STREET LOOKING NORTH, *photographer unknown, plate, July 1886 (USAMHI).*

South Washington Street served as the main artery through Gettysburg for elements of the Union Eleventh Corps en route to the first day's battlefield north of town. This photograph, commissioned by Union veterans in 1886, depicts the street much as it had appeared in 1863, even down to the brick sidewalks (constructed in 1859). Not all of the buildings visible here, however, stood at the time of the battle. Seen to the immediate left of the telephone pole to the left in the modern version is the brick house of Jacob Stock, which still bears numerous battle scars on its southern side.

Modern

2) VIEW FROM THE McPHERSON FARM LOOKING TOWARD SEMINARY RIDGE, *Brady, plate, ca. July 15, 1863 (LC).*

One of only a handful of 1863 photographs taken on the first day's battlefield west of Seminary Ridge, this scene depicts the famous cameraman, M. B. Brady (right foreground), and one of his three assistants, the latter pointing to the woods in which Union General John F. Reynolds had been killed on the morning of July 1, 1863. Reynolds was the highest ranking officer from either side to fall at Gettysburg. It was in the vicinity of the McPherson farm that the main infantry battle began. The cupola of the Lutheran Seminary can be seen in the 1863 photograph, above the trees in the distance.

Modern

3) GETTYSBURG FROM OAK RIDGE,
Henry A. Stewart (amateur), cabinet, 1888 (ACHS).

Taken in 1888 from the right-flank position of the Union First Corps, this scene shows the fields across which many of the Union forces retreated after their defeat on the afternoon of the first day's battle. It will be noted that the figure on the 13th Massachusetts monument (foreground, erected in 1885), was later shifted to face northward. The main building of Pennsylvania College, visible in the distance just above and to the right of the monument, is still standing, but is today obscured from this position by modern structures. The Mummasburg Road can be seen extending into town at the far left.

Modern

4) THE THOMPSON HOUSE, LEE'S HEADQUARTERS,

C. J. Tyson, stereo #573, 1867 (WAF).

The home of widow Mary Thompson in 1863, this building is today a private museum. Confederate General Robert E. Lee spent some time in the house during the battle, though his headquarters complex included a number of tents situated on the camera side of the Chambersburg Pike. While only one photographer, Brady, displayed any interest in the building in 1863, it would remain a popular subject for cameramen from 1867 to the present. Despite bearing an 18th-century date stone, the Thompson house is believed to have been constructed during the early 1830s.

Modern

5) VIEW FROM THE TOWN LOOKING TOWARD THE OAK RIDGE RAILROAD CUT AND THE TATE HOUSE, *Tyson Brothers, plate, August 1863 (GNMP).*

This 1863 scene was recorded looking northwestward along the Chambersburg Pike and toward Seminary or Oak Ridge, with the Oak Ridge Railroad Cut visible in the distance, and the Perry J. Tate house visible to the right. (The Tate house, long since demolished, stood just west of where the U.S. Post Office currently stands.) With the collapse of the Union First Corps' final defensive line on the ridge during the late afternoon of July 1, 1863, Union forces retreated over the ground depicted here, heading for the town and the safety of Cemetery Hill to the south.

Modern

6) THE OAK RIDGE RAILROAD CUT FROM THE TATE HOUSE,

Mumper, stereo, ca. 1882 (LC).

The Oak Ridge Railroad Cut, seen in the center distance, was the only one of the two major cuts on the first day's field to command the interest of photographers for many years after the battle. This previously unpublished view depicts the Oak Ridge Cut, site of the largest mass capture of Union forces at Gettysburg, as it appeared from the Perry J. Tate house. The unfinished railroad embankment, which extended into the town, had served as a main route of retreat for troops of the Union First Corps on July 1, 1863. Because of 20th-century development in this area, the modern companion was recorded from the tracks (finally laid in 1885).

Modern

7) CONFEDERATE PRISONERS ON SEMINARY RIDGE, *Brady, stereo #2397, ca. July 15, 1863 (LC).*

One of the most famous wartime photographs recorded at Gettysburg, this Brady scene depicts three Confederate prisoners on Seminary Ridge, posing adjacent to the Chambersburg Pike on or about July 15, 1863. Judging from the location and date, they were most likely stragglers who had been captured miles west of Gettysburg and during the Confederate retreat. The log breastworks on which they pose had been constructed by Confederate forces on July 4, 1863. The stone wall which currently occupies this site was probably built decades after the war, despite the presence of a plaque which dates it to the time of the battle.

Modern

8) THE LUTHERAN THEOLOGICAL SEMINARY, *Tyson Brothers, plate, August 1863 (GNMP).*

Erected in 1832, the main edifice of the Lutheran Theological Seminary was one of the most imposing structures at Gettysburg in 1863. Its cupola was used as an observatory by Union officers during the first day's fighting, and undoubtedly served the same function for Confederate officers through July 4, 1863. The structure also served as a field hospital for nearly two months after the battle, and is today the home of the Adams County Historical Society. Seminary Ridge, known as Oak Ridge prior to the battle, derived its name from the presence of the Lutheran Theological Seminary.

Modern

9) VIEW LOOKING SOUTHEASTWARD FROM THE CUPOLA OF THE LUTHERAN THEOLOGICAL SEMINARY, *Mumper, cabinet, 1889 (WAF).*

The importance of the Seminary cupola as an observatory is amply illustrated by this Mumper photograph taken looking southeastward toward Gettysburg. Not until the 20th century would the town expand substantially in the direction of Seminary Ridge. Visible beyond the town in the center background of the Mumper scene is Culp's Hill, with East Cemetery Hill and the National Cemetery (heavily foliated with postwar plantings) extending to the right. The Seminary cupola is not open to the public, but a modern, 360-degree series of panoramic photographs, taken from the cupola, is currently on display at the Adams County Historical Society.

Modern

10) GETTYSBURG FROM SEMINARY RIDGE,
C. J. Tyson, stereo #576, 1867 (WAF).

This 1867 C. J. Tyson stereo of Gettysburg, recorded from a camera position on Seminary Ridge adjacent to the Fairfield Road (out of the camera's field of vision to the right), depicts the town essentially as it had appeared four years earlier. The old Millerstown Road, seen dominating the center of the 1867 view, was later removed to facilitate development. The town proper was occupied by Confederate forces from late in the afternoon of July 1 until the early morning hours of July 4, 1863, at which time all of their main lines were temporarily consolidated along Seminary Ridge.

Modern

11) THE ROUND TOPS FROM THE EMMITSBURG ROAD, *A. R. Waud, pencil sketch, July 1863 (LC).*

The actual Confederate positions on Seminary Ridge south of the Fairfield Road attracted virtually no attention from photographers prior to the construction of West Confederate Avenue in the 1890s. Reproduced here is a highly accurate sketch, drawn by the acclaimed Northern artist, Alfred R. Waud, just several days after the battle. It depicts the Round Tops as viewed from the southern portion of the Confederate Seminary Ridge line, where the latter crossed the Emmitsburg Road. Waud, who did not witness any of the fighting from Confederate positions, used artistic license to portray "rebel artillery" in the foreground.

Modern

12) VIEW LOOKING NORTHWESTWARD FROM LITTLE ROUND TOP,
Mumper, cabinet, 1889 (WAF).

Ultimately the key position on the Union left during the second and third days' battles, Little Round Top was ironically unoccupied by combat troops at the time of the initial Confederate advance on the afternoon of July 2, 1863. Because of the timely observations of General G. K. Warren, Union infantry reached the hill just ten minutes or so before the arrival of the Confederates. This Mumper photograph, taken looking toward the Wheatfield Road, clearly illustrates the hill's tactical importance. Despite the presence of several postwar structures, visible along the road in Mumper's scene, the terrain depicted here had changed little since 1863.

Modern

13) GROUP OF EARLY SIGHTSEERS AMID THE BREASTWORKS ON LITTLE ROUND TOP,

P.S. & H.E. Weaver, stereo #91 (negative #129), 1867 (WAF).

The boulder-strewn western face of Little Round Top, with its network of stone breastworks constructed by Union forces during the night of July 2-3, 1863, would quickly emerge as a popular attraction for early photographers and visitors to the battlefield. Depicted here is a group of visitors in 1867, posing at the battle position of the 91st Pennsylvania Infantry. In the center background of the modern companion can be seen the statue of Union General G. K. Warren, erected in 1888. Had Confederate forces been able to capture Little Round Top, and place artillery on its summit, they may have been able to compromise the Union positions on Cemetery Ridge.

Modern

14) THE ROUND TOPS FROM THE J. T. WEIKERT FARM, *C. J. Tyson, stereo #555, 1867 (WAF).*

Taken from the John T. Weikert farm, this photograph portrays both Little Round Top and the more distant Big Round Top as they appeared just four years after the battle. Despite being the smaller of the two hills, Little Round Top possessed substantially greater military value because its western face had been cleared of most of its trees during the years prior to 1863. The hill would remain in Union hands, but only after several hours of bitter fighting on July 2. The marshy ground along the western base of Little Round Top would become known after the battle as the "Valley of Death."

Modern

15) DEVIL'S DEN FROM THE SLAUGHTER PEN, *P. S. Weaver, plate, November 11, 1863 (USAMHI).*

Although the first group of photographers to document the battlefield in July 1863 recorded many death studies in the immediate vicinity of Devil's Den, it would not be until the following November that a local cameraman, Peter S. Weaver, would actually photograph the massive wall of boulders which constituted the Den proper. One of the most revealing scenes from Weaver's 1863 series is reproduced here. It will be noted that numerous boulders were destroyed when the park avenue was constructed through this area. Devil's Den was captured by Confederate forces during the same general assault which failed to secure nearby Little Round Top.

Modern

16) DEAD CONFEDERATES IN THE SLAUGHTER PEN,

Gardner, stereo #265, probably July 6 or 7, 1863 (USAMHI).

The two dead Confederate soldiers seen here in Alexander Gardner's documentation of the Slaughter Pen, situated adjacent to the massive wall of boulders known as Devil's Den, had probably been members of either the 44th or 48th Alabama Infantry, killed during the struggle for the Den on July 2, 1863. The western slope of Little Round Top is obscured in the distance by the atmospheric conditions which often hampered the cameramen during the rainy weather which immediately followed the battle. Long overgrown, much of the Slaughter Pen has been cleared using Gardner's photographs as a guide.

Modern

17) DEAD CONFEDERATE IN THE SLAUGHTER PEN,
Gibson, Gardner stereo #258, probably July 6 or 7, 1863 (LC).

This photograph is a close-up of the same body appearing farthest from the camera in the preceding view. The process of decomposition had already distorted his facial features. A detailed analysis of Gardner's coverage of the battlefield in July 1863 strongly suggests that the identical rifle was often used as a prop to enhance the dramatic effect. And while Gardner frequently described the dead Confederates in this area as "sharpshooters," most if not all had probably been ordinary infantrymen. This soldier, like most of his comrades who were left unburied nearby, would soon be interred in a grave that was probably identified as simply "unknown rebel."

Modern

18) DEAD CONFEDERATE, DEVIL'S DEN, *O'Sullivan, plate, probably July 6 or 7, 1863 (LC).*

One of the most famous photographs recorded at Gettysburg in 1863, this scene was purported by Alexander Gardner to have depicted a dead Confederate sharpshooter who had been killed at his sniper position during the battle. Research by this author was able to prove that the "sharpshooter" was actually an ordinary Confederate infantryman who had been killed 72 yards away, and whose body was carried to this position by the cameramen for dramatic effect. There is even some doubt that the wall depicted here had initially been constructed by and for sharpshooters. The following view depicts the identical soldier at the first location.

Modern

19) DEAD CONFEDERATE, BELOW DEVIL'S DEN,
Gardner, stereo #244, probably July 6 or 7, 1863 (LC).

This photograph is one of six recorded by Gardner's crew of a fallen Confederate soldier, most likely either a Texan or a Georgian, who had been killed during the struggle for the Devil's Den area on the afternoon of July 2, 1863. After spending about an hour with the body at this location, the cameramen decided to carry him 72 yards up the hill, placing him behind a stone enclosure they believed to have been a Confederate sharpshooter's position. The result was the preceding view and a nearly identical companion scene recorded in stereo format.

Modern

20) CONFEDERATE DEAD GATHERED FOR BURIAL AT THE SOUTHWESTERN EDGE OF THE ROSE WOODS,

O'Sullivan, Gardner stereo #245, probably July 5 or 6, 1863 (LC).

Gardner's crew expended twelve negatives on a group of at least 44 dead Confederates at the southwestern edge of the Rose Woods. For more than a century, the connections between the various scenes went unnoticed, with the traditional captions placing individual views at four different locations on the 25-square miles of battlefield. With the author's discovery of the true site in 1967, he was able to establish that all of the dead were Confederates on the Rose farm. The traditional caption for the scene reproduced here misidentified the dead as Union soldiers of the 24th Michigan on the first day's field, three miles from where the scene was actually recorded. Two related views follow.

Modern

21) CONFEDERATE DEAD AT THE SOUTHWESTERN EDGE OF THE ROSE WOODS, *O'Sullivan, Gardner stereo #227, probably July 5 or 6, 1863 (LC).*

Taken just yards from the preceding view, this photograph was traditionally misidentified as Union dead of the 1st Minnesota, men who had been killed fully a mile northeast of where the scene was actually recorded. In reality, the dead—definitely all Confederates—were most likely members of General Paul J. Semmes' Georgia brigade, killed during a successful Confederate counterattack against the Rose Woods on the afternoon of July 2, 1863. Gardner's darkroom wagon, used to process the negative for this and all of the other Gardner photographs taken at Gettysburg, is visible to the far left.

Modern

22) DEAD CONFEDERATE AT THE SOUTHWESTERN EDGE OF THE ROSE WOODS, *O'Sullivan, plate, probably July 5 or 6, 1863 (USAMHI).*

Two negatives were expended on the body depicted here. The photographers, believing that this soldier had been killed by an artillery shell, carefully placed a shell just beyond the soldier's right knee. They also laid the rifle across his legs and probably placed the dismembered hand next to the rifle. Ironically, the author's research has led him to conclude that the massive wound to this soldier's midsection was quite likely the result of animal predation, i.e., by wild hogs. Perhaps no other scene recorded during the entire Civil War depicts the horrors of a battlefield as graphically as does the scene reproduced here.

Modern

23) "THE LOOP," VIEW LOOKING SOUTHWESTWARD TOWARD THE ROSE HOUSE, *Mumper, cabinet, 1889 (WAF).*

The area depicted in this photograph has traditionally been known as "The Loop." Here Union forces, variously comprised of troops from the Third, Fifth, and Second Corps, struggled for several hours during the second day's fighting to stem the relentless Confederate assaults against the Rose Woods. By 1889, when this scene was recorded, most of the trees in this area had been removed, avenues had been constructed, and monuments erected. It is uncertain how Mumper achieved his unusual camera perspective for this photograph. Visible in the far-right distance is the stone farmhouse of John Rose, obstructed from view in the modern companion by the restored woods.

Modern

24) THE WHEATFIELD LOOKING TOWARD THE ROUND TOPS,

Mumper, cabinet, 1889 (WAF).

The scene of chaotic fighting throughout most of the second day's battle on the Union left flank, the Wheatfield would nevertheless go unphotographed until the first monuments began to be erected in this area during the early 1880s. Still, Mumper's photograph of 1889 depicts the Wheatfield much as it had appeared in 1863. It has been estimated that nearly 5,000 soldiers from both sides became casualties in the immediate vicinity of the Wheatfield. By nightfall on July 2, all of the advanced positions on the Union left had been captured by Confederate forces, only Little Round Top (looming in the center distance) serving to stem the Confederate tide.

Modern

25) THE PEACH ORCHARD FROM THE INTERSECTION OF THE EMMITSBURG AND WHEATFIELD ROADS,

Mumper, cabinet, 1889 (WAF).

Like the Wheatfield, most of the Union positions along the Emmitsburg Road, including the Sherfy Peach Orchard (shown here), were largely ignored by photographers prior to the 1880s. This 1889 view of the Peach Orchard was undoubtedly recorded from the rigging used to erect the 63rd Pennsylvania monument that same year. Situated at a point where the advanced line of the Union Third Corps bent sharply northward on July 2, 1863, the salient position at the Peach Orchard was an especially vulnerable one. The original orchard was considerably more extensive than it is today.

Modern

26) VIEW ALONG THE EMMITSBURG ROAD LOOKING SOUTHWESTWARD FROM THE KLINGEL HOUSE,
Mumper, cabinet, 1889 (WAF).

We are here looking southwestward along the Emmitsburg Road and along the advanced line held by the right of the Union Third Corps during the second day's battle. The picket fencing of the Daniel Klingel house dominates the left foreground, with the trees of the Sherfy Peach Orchard being visible in the background. The Joseph Sherfy farm buildings appear to the immediate right of the Emmitsburg Road; and a glimpse of the southern extension of Seminary Ridge, the position from which the Confederate forces launched their assaults, is likewise visible in the far-right background. By July 3, 1863, this portion of the Emmitsburg Road had become part of the main Confederate battle line.

Modern

27) VIEW ALONG THE EMMITSBURG ROAD LOOKING NORTHEASTWARD FROM THE KLINGEL HOUSE, *Mumper, cabinet, 1889 (WAF).*

Taken from the same stretch along the Emmitsburg Road as the preceding view, but now looking in the opposite direction, this Mumper scene shows the lane leading to the Henry Spangler house in the left foreground; the Peter Rogers house (no longer standing) farther down the road on the left; and the postwar barn on the Nicholas Codori farm in the distance (to the right of the Emmitsburg Road). Ziegler's Grove is visible on the horizon, above the Codori barn, while Cemetery Ridge can be seen traversing the right background. It was against the latter portion of Cemetery Ridge that Pickett's Charge was made on the afternoon of the third day's battle.

Modern

28) DEAD ARTILLERY HORSES OF THE 9TH MASSACHUSETTS BATTERY AT THE TROSTLE HOUSE,
O'Sullivan, plate, probably July 6 or 7, 1863 (LC).

With the collapse of the Union Third Corps line on the Emmitsburg Road during the late afternoon of July 2, 1863, Mississippi troops under Confederate General William Barksdale pressed eastward in pursuit. Their advance was temporarily obstructed by the stand of the 9th Massachusetts Battery at the farm of Abraham Trostle, whose house is depicted here in an O'Sullivan photograph recorded just several days after the battle. Numerous artillery horses slain during this encounter are readily visible. It was a common practice for infantrymen attacking an artillery battery to deliberately aim at the horses in order to immobilize the guns.

Modern

29) THE LEISTER HOUSE, MEADE'S HEADQUARTERS, *Tyson Brothers, carte de visite, probably August 1863 (WAF).*

The small farmhouse of widow Lydia Leister, situated on the eastern side of Cemetery Ridge and along the Taneytown Road, was used by the Union commander, General George G. Meade, as his headquarters during the second and third days of the battle. This structure, today restored to its 1863 appearance, suffered damage during the two-hour artillery cannonade which preceded Pickett's Charge on the afternoon of July 3. The cannonade compelled Meade to vacate the building. A shell hole is visible on the right side of the house in this Tyson Brothers scene from 1863.

Modern

30) POWERS HILL AND THE LIGHTNER FARM, VIEW LOOKING SOUTHWARD ALONG THE BALTIMORE PIKE,
Tipton, stereo #712, ca. 1878 (LC).

Powers Hill, seen here looming beyond the farm buildings of Nathaniel Lightner on the Baltimore Pike, served as an important artillery position for Union forces supporting their troops on nearby Culp's Hill. The Lightner farmhouse, seen just beyond the wooden outbuilding in this ca. 1878 photograph, was used as a field hospital during and after the battle. The original stone house still stands today, though it is partially hidden by trees in the modern version. Development along the Pike necessitated that the modern companion be taken from a position closer to the road.

Modern

31) SPANGLER'S MEADOW AT CULP'S HILL, VIEW LOOKING TOWARD POWERS HILL,
Tipton, stereo #514, ca. 1876 (GNMP).

The struggle for Culp's Hill began on the evening of July 2, and continued for seven hours on the morning of July 3, 1863. During the latter portion of the fighting, an ill-conceived counterattack was made by two Union regiments (the 2nd Massachusetts and the 27th Indiana) across the meadow depicted here, known as Spangler's Meadow and situated at the southern base of Culp's Hill. Despite great sacrifice, the charge was doomed. This photograph shows the woods from which the advance was made, as well as Powers Hill in the far distance. The veterans of the 2nd Massachusetts erected a monument at the woodline in 1879—the first such regimental monument to mark a battle position at Gettysburg.

Modern

32) SPANGLER'S SPRING AT CULP'S HILL,
Mumper, cabinet, 1889 (WAF).

One of the enduring legends of the battle was that Union and Confederate soldiers, apparently during an unofficial truce, drank here together from the waters of Spangler's Spring. Although both sides would have had occasion to use the spring, there is no credible evidence that they did so in peaceful harmony (unless prisoners were involved). Despite the fact that Culp's Hill quickly emerged as a popular subject for cameramen, it was not until the 1880s that Spangler's Spring would command their attention. Had Confederate forces pressed their advance in this area on the night of July 2, they may have been able to capture the Baltimore Pike, an important Union supply artery.

Modern

33) UNION BREASTWORKS ALONG GENERAL GREENE'S LINE ON CULP'S HILL,

P.S. & H.E. Weaver, stereo #78 (probably negative #116), 1867 (Stanford).

The popularity of the Culp's Hill area for early visitors and photographers was inextricably related to the physical manifestations of the fighting—notably, acres of shattered trees and an extensive line of Union breastworks—both of which remained for several years along the hill's heavily wooded slopes. Depicted in this rare 1867 scene is a section of the breastworks which had been defended by the 149th New York of Union General George S. Greene's brigade. This brigade, virtually alone, defended Culp's Hill against the Confederate attack on the night of July 2, 1863. Earthen mounds today mark the Union lines in this area.

Modern

34) CULP'S HILL FROM STEVENS KNOLL,
Mumper, cabinet, 1889 (WAF).

This 1889 photograph of Culp's Hill was taken looking northeastward from the Union artillery position at Stevens Knoll. It was from the latter knoll that the guns of Captain G. T. Stevens' 5th Maine Battery fired into the left flank of Confederate forces who unsuccessfully assaulted nearby Cemetery Hill on the evening of July 2, 1863. The modern companion view was recorded from a slightly different camera position because of the presence of the monument to Union General Henry W. Slocum, erected in 1902. Many of the original boulders in the Stevens Knoll area were removed long ago.

Modern

35) EAST CEMETERY HILL FROM STEVENS KNOLL, *Mumper, cabinet, 1889 (WAF).*

Also recorded from Stevens Knoll, this view was taken looking westward toward Cemetery Hill. The Confederate forces which attacked East Cemetery Hill on the evening of the second day's battle advanced from right to left across the open ground in the right distance, and over a stone wall occupied by Union infantry at the base of the hill (note the row of Union monuments at the right). The attack was repulsed, but only after a desperate hand-to-hand struggle near where the wooden observatory stands on the hill's summit in this 1889 scene. Erected in 1878, the observatory was dismantled in 1895. The lane in the near distance has since been shifted slightly.

Modern

36) "THE HIGH WATER MARK OF THE REBELLION," SCENE OF PICKETT'S CHARGE, VIEW LOOKING TOWARD THE ROUND TOPS,

Tipton, stereo #528, 1882 (WAF).

Although the Copse of Trees—situated on Cemetery Ridge where Pickett's Charge was repulsed on the afternoon of July 3, 1863—would eventually come to be regarded as the symbolic "High Water Mark of the Rebellion," it commanded little interest from cameramen prior to the 1880s. Reproduced here is one of the very first photographs recorded specifically of the Copse. This 1882 scene was taken from a platform by William Tipton, who had been commissioned to document the site for Paul Philippoteaux's Gettysburg Cyclorama. In 1863, the Copse of Trees was considerably less distinctive in appearance, being at that time little more than an extensive patch of scrub.

Modern

37) THE BRYAN HOUSE, *Brady, plate, ca. July 15, 1863 (LC).*

One of the only subjects along the Union center on Cemetery Ridge to be photographed in 1863, the farmhouse of Abraham Bryan (a black citizen) was erroneously believed by M. B. Brady to have served as the headquarters of Union General Meade during the battle. Visible in the far-right distance of this Brady photograph is Seminary Ridge and a portion of the open ground over which the left-flank elements of the Confederate forces advanced during Pickett's Charge. The Bryan house may have served as the headquarters of Union General Alexander Hays, whose troops helped to repulse the assault. Though substantially enlarged after the war, the structure has since been restored to its 1863 appearance.

Modern

38) VIEW FROM THE NATIONAL CEMETERY LOOKING TOWARD THE ROUND TOPS,

P. S. Weaver, carte de visite, ca. 1873 (WAF).

This photograph was recorded looking southward toward the distant Round Tops from the southern portion of Cemetery Hill. With the exception of the post-battle cemetery wall and the poplar tree in the foreground, this scene looks much as it did in 1863. Visible to the far left is the wooden barn of Catherine Guinn. Meade's headquarters at the Leister house is partially hidden by the poplar tree; while the Taneytown Road dominates the middle ground. The gentle eastern slope of Cemetery Ridge stretches off to the right. A Union signal station located in the immediate vicinity of the camera position for this photograph was in direct communication during the battle with its counterpart on Little Round Top.

Modern

39) THE MICHIGAN PLOT IN THE NATIONAL CEMETERY, VIEW LOOKING TOWARD EAST CEMETERY HILL, *C. J. Tyson, stereo #508, 1867 (WAF).*

The process of exhuming the more than 3,000 Union dead who remained on the battlefield, and reinterring them into the "Soldiers' National Cemetery," began in October 1863 and was completed the following March. Plans for developing and landscaping the National Cemetery proceeded without regard for the independently conceived project of preserving the battlefield as it appeared in 1863. This 1867 photograph shows a portion of the National Cemetery before the extensive plantings began to obstruct the various vistas. The keeper's lodge visible in the background had been completed by 1865. Improved in 1868, it was completely replaced by the current lodge in 1903.

Modern

40) THE GATEHOUSE AT EVERGREEN CEMETERY,

Tyson Brothers, plate, August 1863 (GNMP).

Cemetery Hill received its name from Evergreen Cemetery, a community burial ground established in the mid-1850s. The gatehouse to Evergreen Cemetery was one of the most distinctive features on the hill at the time of the battle, and hence was one of the most popular subjects for the early photographers. This Tyson Brothers plate of August 1863 was taken looking toward the front of the gatehouse from the portion of East Cemetery Hill that had been defended by Union forces during the Confederate infantry assault on the evening of July 2, 1863. The original gatehouse, despite the addition over the years of more commodious quarters, today remains in a remarkable state of preservation, and is owned by the Evergreen Cemetery Association.

Modern

41) THE NATIONAL CEMETERY ON THE DAY OF THE DEDICATION, TAKEN FROM THE DUTTERA HOUSE ON THE EMMITSBURG ROAD, *P. S. Weaver, plate, November 19, 1863 (HAHS).*

Among the rarest of the rare, this previously unknown and never-before-published photograph by Peter S. Weaver was identified by Weaver as "View of the National Cemetery, taken from the Emmitsburg Road on the 19th of November 1863." The original print, which recently surfaced as a result of the publication of *Early Photography at Gettysburg*, was discovered by Mr. Fred Sherfy in the collections of the Hanover Area Historical Society. One of at least two scenes now believed to have been produced by Weaver that day, this image currently raises the total of known photographs recorded in Gettysburg on November 19, 1863, to nine.

Judging from the camera's perspective in relationship to the rear of the Evergreen gatehouse, it can be deduced that this photograph was taken looking eastward from the back of the William H. Duttera house, which then stood on the eastern side of the Emmitsburg Road. The Taneytown Road can be seen traversing the middle distance (just beyond the carriages and wagons in the foreground); while on the horizon can be clearly distinguished, from left to right: the 90-foot poplar tree on East Cemetery Hill; the Evergreen gatehouse; the flagpole erected for the dedication of the National Cemetery; and to the immediate right of the flagpole, a slight rise indicating the speakers' stand from which President Abraham Lincoln delivered the Gettysburg Address.

The unique spatial relationship between the gatehouse, the flagpole, and the speakers' stand—when compared to the shift in that relationship as evidenced by a careful study of the other photographs taken that day from different perspectives—is consistent with this author's findings in *Early Photography at Gettysburg* as to the site of the speakers' stand from which Lincoln spoke.

The Duttera house (situated in 1863 between the Henry Bishop house and the "Emanuel Trostle" house) was torn down during the mid-1950s, with the original view from the Duttera site currently being obstructed by a motel. The modern companion, therefore, could not be recorded from Weaver's 1863 camera position, and only approximates the same view as it appears today.

The extensively excavated ground visible in the far-left foreground of the 1863 scene may be related to the fact that William H. Duttera was a brickmaker, with his backyard perhaps serving as a source for raw material.

Modern

42) SCENE IN EVERGREEN CEMETERY,
C. J. Tyson, stereo #516, 1867 (WAF).

The interior of Evergreen Cemetery was especially well documented by C. J. Tyson in 1867. This scene was taken looking southwestward from the plot of the McIlhenny family, whose cast-iron fence enclosure dominates the foreground. Most of the hundreds of tombstones which stood in July 1863 survived the fighting and may still be seen today. Indeed, several still bear damage inflicted by Confederate artillery fire, which was often concentrated against Cemetery Hill during the second and third days of the battle. The original iron enclosures were removed in recent years to facilitate mowing.

Modern

43) THE BATTLEFIELD HOTEL AT THE INTERSECTION OF BALTIMORE STREET AND THE EMMITSBURG ROAD, *photographer unknown, plate, July 1886 (LC).*

With the Confederate forces occupying the town of Gettysburg during the second and third days of the battle, the Battlefield Hotel (center; known as the Wagon Hotel in 1863) served as an advanced outpost for Union pickets. Nowhere else in the town were the opposing sides as close to each other as they were at this intersection. Indeed, it was in a house situated just across the street from the left side of the hotel that Jennie Wade was struck by a stray bullet on July 3, 1863, to become the only local civilian killed during the battle. The Emmitsburg Road may be seen extending off to the right, while Baltimore Street continues to the left as it ascends Cemetery Hill. The original hotel was destroyed by fire in 1895.

Modern

44) VIEW FROM GETTYSBURG LOOKING TOWARD EAST CEMETERY HILL, *photographer unknown, stereo, ca. 1873 (WAF).*

Recorded looking southward from a point opposite the German Reformed Church (today the Trinity United Church of Christ) on South Stratton Street, this previously unpublished scene is currently the only pre-1880s photograph of East Cemetery Hill known to have been taken from the town. The view depicts the hill much as it had appeared to the Confederate forces who attacked that position on the evening of July 2, 1863. Clearly visible on the distant summit is the 90-foot poplar tree which stood just across from the gatehouse to Evergreen Cemetery. The wooded area seen in the right foreground of this scene quite likely harbored Confederate sharpshooters during the battle.

Modern

45) BALTIMORE STREET FROM THE SQUARE IN GETTYSBURG,
Mumper, cabinet, 1889 (WAF).

Taken looking southward down Baltimore Street from the square in Gettysburg, this 1889 Mumper photograph depicts the dry goods store of G. W. Spangler to the left, and the dry goods store of John L. Schick to the right. Because of their central location, both buildings were used by relief services during the chaotic days which immediately followed the battle. The original buildings still stand today, each appearing much as it had when first constructed years before the Civil War. The Schick building was one of only a handful of three-story structures in the borough of Gettysburg in 1863.

Modern

46) THE McCLELLAN HOUSE ON THE SQUARE IN GETTYSBURG, *photographer unknown, ca. 1870s (Spectrum).*

Taken looking in the opposite direction from the preceding view, this photograph depicts the McClellan House, one of the oldest hotels in Gettysburg. The structure has been substantially rebuilt and enlarged over the years, and is today known as the Gettysburg Hotel. At the time of the battle, the square (also called the Diamond during that period) was an open area and the site of much confusion during the retreat of Union forces through the town on the afternoon of July 1, 1863, especially since the troops were pouring in from both the west and the north. The park-like island in the center of the square was constructed in 1918.

Modern

47) PENNSYLVANIA COLLEGE,
C. J. Tyson, stereo #509, 1867 (WAF).

Pennsylvania College, officially known as Gettysburg College since 1921, was founded in 1832 and helped to prepare many students for the nearby Lutheran Theological Seminary. The main edifice of the college was constructed in 1837 and can be seen here, looming above the trees in C. J. Tyson's photograph of 1867. During the battle, the cupola of this imposing Greek Revival structure was used as an observatory, with the building itself serving as a field hospital for several weeks. Former students of Pennsylvania College served in the ranks of both armies at Gettysburg, and several were listed among the casualties.

Modern

48) THE ADAMS COUNTY ALMS HOUSE ON THE HARRISBURG ROAD,

Tipton, plate, ca. 1885 (GNMP).

Because so few early photographs were recorded on the first day's field north of town, this scene depicting the Adams County Alms House on the old Harrisburg Road is of special interest. The complex of brick buildings was established before the Civil War to provide shelter for the county's poor, incapacitated, and insane. One of the most distinctive features on the Union right during the fighting of July 1, 1863, the Alms House also served as a field hospital. The complex was dismantled during the 1960s. Located just beyond is Barlow's Knoll, where the line of the Union Eleventh Corps began to break on the first day.

Modern

49) THE YORK PIKE STONE BRIDGE OVER ROCK CREEK, VIEW FROM THE RAILROAD LOOKING TOWARD CULP'S HILL,

Tipton, stereo #858, 1880s (WAF).

One of the more obscure subjects photographed by William Tipton during the 1880s, the old Rock Creek bridge on the York Pike (constructed in 1807 at the eastern edge of the borough) was typical of many of the spans which crossed the creeks of Adams County at the time of the battle. The railroad bridge located to the right of the camera position for this view was burned by the Confederates a few days before the battle. Of all of the original bridges in the immediate vicinity of the battlefield, only one—the Sachs Covered Bridge over Marsh Creek (near the Eisenhower Farm)—has been preserved, thanks in large part to the efforts of the Gettysburg Battlefield Preservation Association.

Modern

50) THE EAST CAVALRY BATTLEFIELD FROM THE SPANGLER HOUSE ON THE HANOVER ROAD,
P. S. Weaver, stereo, ca. mid-1870s (Schwartz).

The final scene to be reproduced here is the earliest known photograph of the East Cavalry Battlefield, taken looking northward from the second story of the Joseph Spangler house on the Hanover Road. The original Spangler house still stands three miles east of Gettysburg, but is currently in such dilapidated condition that the modern companion was made from the front yard. Fortunately, the structure was recently acquired by the National Park Service, and plans are underway to consider a restoration. Visible in the distance of this rare photograph is the farm of Jacob Lott, with an extensive woods located just beyond. It was generally along a line running from the Spangler house to these woods that Union cavalry, facing to the left, met and repulsed their Confederate counterparts on the afternoon of July 3, 1863. Together with Pickett's Charge, this cavalry action effectively signaled the end of the actual battle at Gettysburg.

Modern

NOTES

Of the 50 historical scenes selected for inclusion in this study, only two were reproduced from the identical prints used in *Early Photography at Gettysburg* (*EPG*); and only seven were made from the identical prints used in *Gettysburg: A Journey in Time* (*Journey*). The latter books, which contain a total of some 500 photographs, are different from each other, with *EPG* being more extensive in scope than *Journey*, and reflecting 20 years of additional research.

Because both *EPG* and *Journey* go into much greater detail concerning many of the subjects depicted in *Gettysburg: Then and Now*, and often include companion scenes not reproduced herein, I have added the following notes for those who would like to learn more by referring to the appropriate sections in *EPG* and *Journey*. Both *EPG* and *Journey* are available through your local bookstore or from Thomas Publications of Gettysburg, Pa.

2) *EPG*, pp. 56-59; *Journey*, pp. 64-67.
4) *EPG*, pp. 64-66; *Journey*, pp. 72-73.
5) *EPG*, pp. 81-84.
6) *EPG*, pp. 68-73.
7) *Journey*, pp. 70-71.
8) *EPG*, pp. 66-67; *Journey*, pp. 78-79.
10) 1863 versions of this scene will be found in *EPG*, pp. 73-81; *Journey*, pp. 80-81.
11) For more on Waud's Gettysburg sketches, see *EPG*, pp. 103-107; *Journey*, pp. 182-183.
12) For other scenic views from Little Round Top, see *EPG*, pp. 252-255, 258-266; *Journey*, pp. 156-157.
13) 1863 versions of this scene will be found in *Journey*, pp. 162-163.
14) For other views of the Round Tops from similar perspectives, see *EPG*, pp. 242-246; *Journey*, pp. 154-155.
15) The entire Weaver series of November 11, 1863, including posed "dead," will be found in *EPG*, pp. 294-306; see also *Journey*, pp. 184-185.
16-17) The Slaughter Pen death studies, including additional scenes, are discussed in *EPG*, pp. 279-294; *Journey*, pp. 172-181.
18-19) For details concerning the movement of the dead "sharpshooter," including additional scenes, see *EPG*, pp. 268-278; *Journey*, 186-195.
20-22) The Rose farm death studies, including additional scenes, are detailed in *EPG*, pp. 319-350; *Journey*, pp. 196-221.
28) *Journey*, pp. 148-149.
29) *EPG*, pp.219-224; *Journey*, pp. 144-145.
31) This scene and two companions were previously thought to have been taken ca. 1866, see *Journey*, pp. 136-139; corrected in *EPG*, pp. 232, 420.
33) For other views related to the Union breastworks and the shattered trees on Culp's Hill, see *EPG*, pp. 195-209; *Journey*, pp.128-133.
34-35) *EPG*, pp. 195-200; *Journey*, pp. 106-107.
36) A discussion of the early lack of interest in photographing the site of the climax of Pickett's Charge, together with the earliest known views, will be found in *EPG*, pp. 234-240.
37) *EPG*, pp. 229-234; *Journey*, pp. 146-147.
38-39) *EPG*, pp. 169-192; *Journey*, pp. 122-123.
40) *EPG*, pp. 146-152; *Journey*, pp. 108-111.
41) The most extensive discussion of the photographic coverage of the dedication of the National Cemetery on November 19, 1863, with additional views, will be found in *EPG*, pp. 128-135, 160-167; see also *Journey*, pp. 116-121.
42) *EPG*, pp. 153-159.
43) *EPG*, pp. 119-135; *Journey*, pp. 94-97, 116-117.
45-46) Additional photographs taken on the square will be found in *EPG*, pp. 92-98; *Journey*, pp. 86-87.
47) *EPG*, pp. 107-111; *Journey*, pp. 82-83.
50) Weaver's original handwritten description of this scene was "From the Spangler House showing the Lott House and where the skirmish was between Stuart & McIntosh & some other brigades."

William A. Frassanito has been studying Gettysburg and the Civil War since the age of nine. He graduated from Gettysburg College in 1968 and received his master's degree in American cultural history from the State University of New York at Oneonta. As a first lieutenant in the U. S. Army, he served as an intelligence analyst for the Joint General Staff in Vietnam and was awarded the Bronze Star. He is also the author of *Gettysburg: A Journey in Time*; *Antietam: The Photographic Legacy of America's Bloodiest Day*; *Grant and Lee: The Virginia Campaigns*; *The Gettysburg Bicentennial Album;* and *Early Photography at Gettysburg*. Mr. Frassanito has served as the chief photographic consultant to numerous projects, including the National Historical Society's six-volume photo history of the Civil War, *The Image of War*; and Time-Life Books' twenty-eight-volume series, *The Civil War*. He has appeared in a number of television broadcasts and lives in Gettysburg, Pennsylvania.

Books by William A. Frassanito and available from Thomas Publications:

Gettysburg: A Journey in Time
Antietam: The Photographic Legacy of America's Bloodiest Day
Grant and Lee: The Virginia Campaigns
Early Photography at Gettysburg